Excavations

WINNERS OF THE SOUTH CAROLINA POETRY BOOK PRIZE

Keep and Give Away
Susan Meyers

Driving through the Country before You Are Born
Ray McManus

Signals
Ed Madden

How God Ends Us
DéLana R. A. Dameron

Excavations: A City Cycle
Jennifer R. Pournelle

Excavations
A City Cycle

Jennifer R. Pournelle

Foreword by Rigoberto González

THE UNIVERSITY OF SOUTH CAROLINA PRESS

*Published in Cooperation with the South Carolina Poetry Initiative,
University of South Carolina*

Published by the University of South Carolina Press
Columbia, South Carolina 29208

www.sc.edu/uscpress

Manufactured in the United States of America

20 19 18 17 16 15 14 13 12 11   10 9 8 7 6 5 4 3 2 1

Library of Congress Cataloging-in-Publication Data

Pournelle, Jennifer R.
   Excavations : a city cycle : poems / Jennifer R. Pournelle.
      p. cm.
   "Published in cooperation with the South Carolina Poetry Initiative,
University of South Carolina."
   ISBN 978-1-61117-008-5 (pbk : alk. paper)
   1. Cities and towns—Poetry. I. Title.
   PS3616.O869E93 2011
   811'.6—dc23

                                                        2011032537

The South Carolina Poetry Book Prize is given annually to the manuscript that
wins the contest organized and sponsored by the South Carolina Poetry Initiative.
The winning title is published by the University of South Carolina Press in co-
operation with the South Carolina Poetry Initiative.

For Yvonne

As a writer, one is busy with archaeology.

Michael Ondaatje,
interview with Ellen Kanner

Contents

Foreword

Shelley's famous sonnet "Ozymandias" is also known as one of the earliest poems in the English language to contain allusions to an archaeological dig. The speaker comes upon a traveler who describes a ruin and who concludes from his visit that no empire (and, by association, no emperor) stands forever. And yet, because the traveler has also become the storyteller, one could argue that the empire—and the neglected narrative of its leader—has been resurrected by the listener's imagination. It now appears as but a ghost of itself, and so it must be mourned. But it has also come to teach us about loss, mortality, vulnerability, and humility, and so its lessons must be learned.

Echoes of Shelley's poem haunted me as I read through the pages of Jennifer Pournelle's *Excavations: A City Cycle,* where a traveler guides the reader through distinct landscapes, each one set ablaze by a rich culture and architecture and darkened by political and religious turmoil. That is how we know we encounter greatness in a city: when its bittersweet history hovers above it as large and loud as the clear sky.

The excavations that take place in this book are literal and metaphorical. As the speaker moves through Europe, the American Southwest, and the Middle East, she is undertaking a serious study of the brick-and-mortar composition of cities such as Vienna, Berlin, San Diego, and Baghdad. But each city is, as the speaker notes, "a city within a city," that is, a story within a story, the layers of which come to light as the speaker soaks up each environment—its textures, its temperatures, its temperaments—its past offenses, its present troubles, and its future possibilities:

> There is a city under the city.
> It sucks and turns in byways that crash through new
>   foundations
> chapels breaking vault-first into subway tunnels
> spilling ochre-yellow light and finger-painted walls
> onto the underground feet of tourists
> stumbling lost in confrontation with a foreign city
>   unmapped
>   unknown and unreported
>   unlisted in the guidebooks

The word for a narrative showing through another is *palimpsest*, and world history is full of such examples. When one nation invades another and asserts its colonial presence, a great change comes to a place and to the people who inhabit it. There is also the aggressive act of erasure, when a dominant ethnic, religious, or political group attempts to bury another group. And perhaps the most painful act of all is progress, when new ideas, new technologies, new gestures of creativity, displace the old-fashioned, the outdated—the brittle artifacts now considered obsolete, which, if not recovered or recorded are doomed to disappear into the deadness of forgetting:

> There's a city over the city.
> Construction cranes pick at the rubble of backstreet courts
> wading through the lapping graffiti tide
> where all that should be electrified
> waits for lightening rods to earth the tensions
> ionized along steaming compost fumes rising from ruined
>   cellars
> where bodies piled and disavowed
> lay rotting low these many years

            no one left to remember
            how explosive gasses are manufactured into fertilizer
        no one left to remember
        the flutter of other mothers' shawls.

By speaking to us about the lessons unearthed in other cities, the speaker has better prepared us (or so she hopes) to learn how to navigate—and maybe save—the ravaged cities of the Middle East, the most contemporary examples of history and culture under siege, of beauty collapsing under the weight of the ugly. Unlike the dissemination of information in the past, in the present this knowledge is received almost instantaneously, and we bear witness as acts of destruction unfold. Through television or the Internet, we have indeed reached the quick-access stage of globalization, and therefore we should react immediately. But we do not. And if we do, the response is just as damaging:

                There's a city around this city:
                A city of industry and landfills;
                glass factories and furniture repairs;
                a dying city, a trying city,
                a city under attack, assault, explosions.

Perhaps this is the sad truth about Shelley's sonnet first published in 1818. Almost two centuries later, humanity is not wiser—more knowledgeable, for sure, but knowledge does not necessarily translate into wisdom. And yet we keep building and building, even with the rubble of our own undoing:

                And where the city lives, we live,
                and eat and sing and drink and laugh,
                and love, and war, and cry.

And that is where Jennifer Pournelle comes in, so too the urgency of this sobering book, as an energy that brings together what our Babylonian existence pulls apart, as an antidote to the romanticizing of tourism (which only takes and does not give) or to the exoticizing of foreignness or difference (never seeing beyond the two dimensions). An honest sense of responsibility takes hold of the pages of this book. Like the traveler in "Ozymandias," the speaker in Pournelle's *Excavation: A City Cycle* takes note of her experience and challenges us with complexity. What will you, dear reader, do with the constructions you now hold in your hands?

This is not unlike the numerous exchanges between Marco Polo and Kublai Kahn in another literary masterpiece, Italo Calvino's *Invisible Cities:* one travels and one remains stationary, one speaks and the other listens, both play the architect and the archaeologist, and together they rebuild structures that will remain standing, indeed indestructible, in the imagination.

What is loss, then, when there exists this saving grace called recovery? What can disappear if we don't exercise memory? And whose responsibility is it to collect the broken pieces and put them together again? Pournelle poses these critical questions to those of us who know that devastation is inevitable, conflict is unstoppable, but so too healing and—dare we dream it—the potential to one day be able keep our precarious house-of-cards civilizations intact. But in the meantime this vision, to rebuild with the shards we still hold sacred . . .

> like light from far-flung stars arriving now so brilliantly,
> so long and far away from where the stars themselves
>   blinked out.

Rigoberto González

Acknowledgements

I am grateful to the United States Army Foreign Area Officer Fellows Program, the University of California Institute on Global Conflict and Cooperation and Office of Research, the National Science Foundation, and the United States Agency for International Development. All provided me with the opportunity for advanced studies and work in very interesting places during very interesting times.

I am grateful to Charlene Spearen for sparing time from her overwrought schedule to provide advice and encouragement.

And, always, I am grateful to Yvonne Ivory, who has lived through it all with me, and who reminded me daily that art is what makes life worth living.

Finally, grateful acknowledgement is made to the editors of the following journals in which these poems first appeared:

Parnassus Literary Journal: "Babylon"
Minerva: "Jerusalem"

Vienna

Karlsplatz Underground

Vienna, 1989

Here in the hours before the air has curled asleep
Women pass by
Hard as grimy water sloshed grey across ashen marble floors
Their grimy rags slopped along the steps
The hands that wring them bitter with the shabby air of
    cigarette butts
        shuffled by the pounding feet
        grinding heavy across their scrubbing lives.

The Excavation of Saint Michael's Square

Vienna, 1989

I

We scrambled over crumbled brick,
kitchen ash and mortar dust,
ground to paste by cartwheels
and plastered in the cellar arches
packed with mud and sawdust swept from shop floors
and scattered to the breeze from windows leaning out above
    the market crowds.

Walled in and scrambled over
       yellow-shirted students clips and pens in hand
       sketching the terrain
       subterranean
       paved over
       rumbled above
       chattering with cartwheels
shuddering with the stammer of sewer pipes and storm drain
    sludge
       jackhammers mobilized
       bulldozers
       bare-backed Turkish engineers, shovels in hand

three weeks to excavate a millennium—
better done with toothpicks and camel-hair brushes—
three weeks to poke edgewise in the rubble
and follow echo-traces of gentle voices
calling down alleyways better filled with open air.

II

There is a city under the city.
It sucks and turns in byways that crash through new foundations
chapels breaking vault-first into subway tunnels
spilling ochre-yellow light and finger-painted walls
onto the underground feet of tourists
stumbling lost in confrontation with a foreign city
        unmapped
        unknown and unreported
        unlisted in the guidebooks
street plans running counter to the lay of imperial courts above
dust heaps burying pocket change and shards of last week's
    milk jugs
underlying the stock exchanges, Christmas markets, and
    marble pillars on the Freyung.

III

We burrowed under our city
expecting to find the street plan for roads that rumble above
instead, slammed into walls and dodged children tossing
    pebbles in the lane—
explorers, potholers, spelunkers we,
we combed the tunnels and found our highways
undercut by boreholes lined with rail sparks;
were forced to detour around real fundaments
that anchor open air to bedrock
fertile goddesses on the lintels smiling open-lipped at passersby
    oblivious to modern morals
extending legs toward open grain bins
and calling open air back down into the storehouses—
    oblivious to modern words
virgin Madonnas beckoning from the walls,
milk geysers gushing from their breasts,
suckling wide-eyed infant Christs,
resurrecting infant cities,
guiding us to praise the cool,
scrape free the dust,
shake off our shirts under the open sky,

run our fingers through thousand-year groats,
flash our teeth at bulldozer drivers,
and grip rough-handled shovels to revel in the grime
our shoulders heaving and breasts burning in the sun.

IV

There is a city under the city.
It is scratched beneath the print of postcards we write dutifully
    home.
It is waved in the evening smog and wadded in the gutters
by red-and-yellow-coated vendors whose cries echo the
    defiance
of women wailing above the ancient walls
once tumbled by angry trumpet blasts from dreary classroom
    doorways
then shaken into coma by the dreary tramp of jackboots.

The headlines caption their dance upon new barriers as,
        our hearts rocking with the terror of their heights;
        our hearts rocking with the terror of the fall,
we peer down at the city gates,
at the cascading dust and intruding lights,
at dark fists smearing newsprint into sleep-black faces;
into mug-shot poses of former masters sweating in the heat
trembling glassy-eyed before the chanting market crowds
who search the walls for crumbling stone and open air

the pattering rain of feet washing away the marching echoes
their fingers prying; ripping crevices,
      handholds,
      footholds,
      chimney grips;
chisels raised, instead of scythes
to play tattoo and taps upon the concrete slabs
that topple rootless into open arms below.

V

We peer wide-eyed from our narrow embrace
search walls laid bare of ivy with our faces
suckle at one another's breasts
grow drunk on one another's lips
wonder at our heaving chests
feast on thousand-year bread
wonder that we cannot make our way
and find that the dark and dusty city above the city
no longer exists at excavation's end.

Berlin

Berlin, in Germany Reunified

Berlin, 1991

I

There's a city over the city.
It flies to us in airwaves that unite Red Square and the mayor of
    Leningrad
with the crumbling balconies of Prenzlauer Berg,
where scaffolding and pastel paint
rain down upon coal-dusted facades care-worn in the traffic-
    choked turnings
past heaving chunks of stucco jettisoned from political ramparts
that once set shipbuilders at techno-cruisers,
then abandoned to drift the masted wrecks
of programs begun under other governments.

II

Flag-draped coffins pass from hand to hand,
no passing mourned but sung, rejoiced in Church Slavonic,
and wafted in the scents of myrrh
packed in from sister cities sweating in Africa,
their sharp-faced mothers wrapped in shawls so very white,
landing in airplanes chartered for freight
diverted from intended landing sites.

We hover, looking up for bearings over the rubble mountains
        met by none, greeted by all
staggering along the corridors
passage directed by yellow-stained circles in the armpits of
    Bombay businessmen
not lost as we in this bazaar of snarling ancient trade routes,
the memories of sharp-faced mothers
marking passageways to a past we never learned.

III

There's a city over the city.
We heave and sweat,
our writing obsolete before the pen can cross a page;
we struggle to recognize paved, grassed-over traces
of clearer lines that marked the city's boundaries before we
      began our ascent,
helicopters outpaced by bankrupt airlines,
their lumbering jumbo jets no match in speed
for the news each night of singing republics,
passed from hand to hand.

Our hands unite.
Instead of courage drunk on barricades,
the righteous sing a mass in praise of a history that should have
      been,
when glass never rained in sparkling shards
amid the dust of balconies cascading down onto the heads of
      passersby.

IV

We say to ourselves our love was right
and look out across each square that once echoed in parade-
    field lines,
now softened by the whispers of departing soldiers who sing
    and cry—
incomprehensible the polar circle they'll follow home
landing in a place they've never seen—
we've never been—
where lines are babbled in the airwaves
food stalls, shop queues, and parliaments
bubbled, rippled, shaken, snapped
like shawls fluttering in the breeze
pinned to laundry lines for tightrope walkers
who dance above the scaffolding,
skipping across the antennas that march black in lines across
    the sky
high above the flaming arcs of Molotovs
that follow tracers left by carpet bombs
laid down in times now erased by the vapor trails of cities in
    the air
that freely trade economic miracles past those gutted cells

burned to their load-bearing walls
and looted to post-war charred wallpaper.

Plastered over
    hidden
    covered
    never spoken of
until flaming arcs light up the night
as signal flares marking memories never handed down—
dead thoughts buried, sullen below the leaden sky,
hatred flickering like a memory across the backs of refugees
burned alive in the shells of their final refuge,
hate's hot white breath steaming through the oily clouds,
the crisp white breath of frozen memory
inhaled in one communal draw.

V

There's a city over the city.
Construction cranes pick at the rubble of backstreet courts
wading through the lapping graffiti tide
where all that should be electrified
waits for lightening rods to earth the tensions
ionized along steaming compost fumes rising from ruined
    cellars
where bodies piled and disavowed
lay rotting low these many years
        no one left to remember
        how explosive gasses are manufactured into fertilizer
no one left to remember
the flutter of other mothers' shawls.

San Diego

Coscoy, Renamed San Diego de Alcala, 1602

San Diego, 1993–96

I

There's a city within the city
Where Kumeyaay sifted tidal silt for clambakes;
pounded river bark to ribbons dyed with purple shells and
    desert ochres;
marked their lips with colors strained from cactus flowers
and traded heavy baskets loaded high with salt-dried fish
for Chumash drugs and palm hearts; prickly pear and acorn
    flour;
for gourds aslosh with sour mescal, the pounding, kneading,
    rolling, scraping
of stone on stone and palms on bread
in tempo with the washing tides to mark the days and hours;
Baskets woven,
bark skirts beaded,
hair roped and larded,
caves and cliffs and rocky faces
painted with the wheels of heaven;
with cycles, suns, and stars—

II

There's a city within the city
even within this city,
laid stucco wall to stucco wall
on grizzled earth scraped clean as seabeds
newly planed to lifelessness by shrimpers' nets.
Where Cabrillo stood on Coscoy's mounds
above reed-choked marshes soon to be malarial
and Fra Serra planted first his Spanish cross—
here, where traffic flows like water never roared,
the slow and brackish estuary
chuffing green beneath the freeway trusses
like light from far-flung stars arriving now so brilliantly,
so long and far away from where the stars themselves blinked
    out—

III

There's a city within the city,
where missions, tiled and stuccoed, rose;
immense adobe barracks, square as Karak citadel,
built in triumph once the Moors seized Palestine,
flash-flooding west as conquerors on stone-paved Roman roads,
a relentless dust storm lashing hard,
blown across North Africa,
their plows replacing Spanish plows;
their colored tiles and Arabesques
and plaster, brilliant white on softening domes,
encrusting Roman villa courts;
their horses, foreheads marked with stars,
plunging past the pagan horns of fighting bulls
beneath the flashing pants of Catholic picadors—

IV

There's a city within the city
here, where soldiers, priests, and farmers
with no need of cities, acorn groves, or clam nets
first plowed-under coastal scrub for buildings,
then plowed down their makeshift walls and kicked aside shell
    middens
for the fortress carried brick by brick within their heads along
    Crusader marches,
struggling against the Indians
compressing at the speed of light a thousand years of city
    growth
to half a century here.

Here, where rivers slog their brackish way
to vast, undrinkable lapping seas;
       to Dead Seas,
       Red Seas,
blue as mosque tiles against the chaparral dust,
here, forests—

submerged and wavering browns of kelp beds tiled with
    abalone,
no use in crafting ship masts or hulls—
here, finally
halting Moors and Crusaders both—

V

There's a city within this city,
in this hostile place so welcome; known;
salt and scent enticing officers; reformers; revolutionary
    guards
to build a home away from home
then plot in darkened houses to upset the status quo
and break the chain that stretched across vast oceans
from their legionary outpost here to Jordan's citadels;
their campaigns beset by fevers
loaded with the cattle, wheat, and corn, and goats
amassed in holds with Canton silk and Plymouth tea
all dumped at dockside, then dispersed
to stud the land with life regrown
in farmer's plots and stick-plowed fields
atop the strip-mined desert soil—

VI

There's a city within this city,
here, the citadels abandoned
for the market gardens, shipping docks, and garrisons
all set alongside royal bells
to mark new causeways north and south—
letters, baggage, governments,
all flashing past on stage stops,
the clattering of the teamsters' hooves
echoing through the warehouses;
the marshes drained to riverbeds,
the rivers dammed and waters sucked
to olive roots, alfalfa fields;
to vineyards, herds, and greenhouses;
sent gushing over citrus groves.
Flowering almonds from Jordan's hills on these hills now,
their petals witness to railroad spurs,
then rails,
then stations;
then concrete spires and stucco towers,

raised above the charnel strips
left by brush fires whipping mules and horses,
      burros, ghettos,
      fields and ghost towns
      grasslands, homes
spilling onto back lots,
engulfing movie sets;
replayed in news clips every summer's end—

VII

There's a city within this city,
this city once raised up,
then pulled back down again,
the flash of starlight winking out,
but excavated still from trash heaps:
      bath tiles,
       broken shards of Fiesta plates
resurrected bright in stucco spires
of rebar filigreed with arabesques and Byzantine mosaic—

Through all of this, the waters flowed;
the adz and plow and bulldoze blade
following on the slower wax of sunlight
glinting past from miners pans and fishers' baskets
out into the Moorish court of seas,
arriving only now on Roman shores;
the sighs of waves not sighs at all,
but washing hands rocked back and forth;
but woven baskets stirred and swayed
to separate the day from weed—

VIII

There's a city within the city.
It beats alive in shrimpers' hearts
with hearty mounds of seabed scraped
from light-years past and roasted, steamed, piled into mouths
at seafood feasts in stucco style,
served up by children hence long mixed
of conquering and conquered—
still tending squash-sprawled gardens
far below the midden mounds;
still trading foodstuffs east and south,
and strolling hand to hand through shopping malls
the cactus colors of their lips; the desert ochres of their caves
kiln-fired across the Spanish tiles
encrusted over Anglo courts erected here in angles; towers;
in mezzanines and breezeways lined
with shop doors hawking Canton silks,
and English teas in linen bags, and holograms, and plastic
    purple carryalls—

It bolts across the freeway lanes
traversing estuary reeds,

comes north on causeways loaded down
with woven cloth, not beaten flat from river bark
but spun from fibers traded here from ship holds;
dyed in wild pastels stuccoed high on deco walls,
the kiss of native cactus lips
the art of Chumash shaman hands
the seed and sex and wealth and eyes still coming here from
distant lands so long since lost to time—

IX

There's a city within the city.
It's sanitized in Old Town;
bastardized and vilified on Avenida Revolucion;
it whirls in bright Casino lights, new stars winked on above
the wheels of chance that spin and tempt
in gaming halls and Indian saloons;
it stares at us from muleteer eyes
caught burning black in daguerreotype;
we catch its smell in lard-soaked stands
that sell fish tacos, freshly spritzed with lime.

The city here that burns within beckons fresh from gallery
    doors;
it lies exposed in fossil seams that mark the ancient midden
    mounds;
it glimmers in the neon signs and hangs in braids on blond
    girls' backs;
it crashes in the concert halls
and dances on the table tops to Mariachi bands—

X

There's a city within the city.
And where the city lives, we live,
and eat and sing and drink and laugh,
and love, and war, and cry;
we tender oceanic nets, imagining like kelp beds that
we feel the movement of the spheres,
so now, built up from all that was,
we are,
like commentary tales that come
from planetary depths long gone.

On Having a Fever

San Diego, 1996

Is this how intrepid travelers
lost, wet, hot, malarial
passed the equatorial night?
Wrapped in red-eyed sleeplessness?
Determined that those who waited at home
should elevate their simple suffering,
well-fed and well-attended,
to a state of colonial grace?

Babylon

Babylon

Heidelberg, 1991

There is no quiet in this evening-peaceful valley
When the stars burn over Baghdad.
Rockets crash past barge lights on the river
When the skies blaze over Baghdad.
Tank turbines grumble through our evening bread
Jet fuel stinks
Iraqi bellies growl
And slack-jawed ghosts
Tramp senseless toward the church spires
To meet the massing shades of Babylon.

Jerusalem

Jerusalem, 1993

The crack of a rifle
The crack of a bone

As if hammering a small boy's arm
with the very rock he threw—
his face twisted in a cowl of tears;
the hammerer, at twice his size,
a mask of earnest endeavor—

As if hammering, the thudding dull
        before the crack along the arm
were work: enduring, new, profound:
a way of mending torn up stones
a way of mending pounded arms
a way of mending lungs torn hot
from busloads by fanatic arms:
wired to detonators, pinned to ribs,
their last, wet break a bloody implosion;
        a crack,
        a spring,
        and then a roar,
and then no sound.

Ramallah

Ramallah, 1994

I

There's a city across from The City
The remnants of biblical olive groves
now suburban trees,
cordoned off within suburban yards:
small plaques left to mark where asses stood:
the asses' pause now hallowed ground.

Yes, beyond the tourist-traveled walls:
Another city, another language
Another time, not biblical
Its dirty streets and traffic snarls
Untempered by more regulated growth
Its lifelines cut:
no taxicabs or satellites.

No crossing points allowed.

II

There's a city across from The City.
Cut off, but still it grows, and manufactures life
from the cast-off dust of its own feet—
          a city poured from secular concrete
          not stacked; preserved; of sacred stone.
A howl of industry—
          no ladders here,
          left long unstowed
          amid caretakers' bickering
          over possession of the past.
The winking lights of Christmas trees
Lost amidst the coil of street lights, hastily-strung.

III

There's a city across from The City
its shirts' arms
bear marks of sweat unsterilized;
bear smells of bus rides on a long commute
the diesel fumes that meet the grey
well before each working dawn
commingling with the sickly sweet
of cheap cologne and disinfectant.

IV

There's a city across from The City.
It holds no grace, it bears no charm
except the grace of greeting
except the charm of struggling
      the food hot,
      the tables hard,
      the lunch fast
      the coffee long
fortifying a scheming, struggling hope

past empty quarters

past wailing walls.

Twin Towers, Viewed from a Hotel Lobby

Baku, Azerbaijan, 9 / 11 / 2001

I

To the towers
Falling; free-falling
Diving headfirst through the burning fires of hell
I freefall into the eye of God.
I see before me beckoning houris
Waving me in
Waving me off
Waving me through a long sparkling tunnel.

A flick of the wrist,
A long day of terror
The heat of the fire melting my resolve;
A flick of the wrist,
And feet flailing
My ankles preceding my bladder
I make my leap of faith and fall free.
Of my own free will fall free,
And freefall into the circling eye of God.

II

From the towers
Falling; free-falling
Escaping the burning fires of hell
I leap into the eye of God.
I see below me beckoning angels
Waving me down
Waving me off
Waving me through a long, rushing tunnel.

A flick of the wrist,
A long moment of terror
The heat of the fire firming my resolve;
A flick of the wrist,
And knees flailing,
My bladder preceding my ankles,
I make my leap of faith and fall free
of my own free will:
Fall free, and freefall
Into the circling eye of God.

Baghdad

Baghdad, When a Church Is Bombed

Baghdad, 2004

I

There is a city around this city
where glass rains down,
splattering shards in cobalt drops across the dusty steps
the haggard eyes of witnesses
red-rimmed, blackened, staring,
fists balled,
throats hoarse from shouting at the sky,
from begging God to stop the rain.

II

There's a city around this city,
its rings of squatters camps
long since leveled,
        sown with salt,
        rebuilt in regulated rows;
reordered into neatened grids
of cinder blocks in modernizing city schemes—
old byways, turning in adobe bends
toward the leafy cool of shaded canal-side gardens,
now erased in one bold sweep of urban engineering.
Rings gone,
the grids, the straight long streets
        now turning nowhere,
        leading nowhere,
encircling all the same,
with a prowling hope imported from the long-gone squatters
   camps without,
now a marching, lockstep ache within.

III

There is a city around this city:
it hides,
it shields,
it breathes a desperate grasp for turnings,
coolness,
a place along the Tigris banks,
a place no more outside,
a place no more The Arab Street;
a place no more the clothes, the speech
the furious and futile pride
of a second city
a made city
a city forced and framed from rural remnants still despised
and now displaced by space and time
from old ancestral lands and ways.

IV

There is a city around this city.
It shuttled once from night to night
in black sedans:
>   black cars,
>   hot cars,
>   big cars,
>   red cars,
>   four-wheel armored SUVs,
>   red sports coupés;
in battered, beaten, orange-and-white-and-dented rusty
    taxicabs—
shuttled, roared, crept, sped,
through the beaten, brutal nights
from Palace moat to Palace basement;
from torture cells to satin beds.

Today, it chokes,
a smog of fear

hovering along the concrete ribbons
        that ring and cross and exit,
        but never, never leave—
that hang above,
a dusty pall along horizon hinterlands.

V

There's a city around this city.
War rooms, tents, and offices;
        HummVs,
        EWACs,
        Tactical Commands;
a soldier-city, a city of soldiers,
they hover, glide, ride, patrol,
surround, transgress, withdraw:
a web, a cage, a deliverance from thirst;
distractions; terrors,
a band of brothers;
a company of friends.
A city they are too,
of crime and hope, and fear and boredom;
of jobs well done, and duties shirked
as many, and as variable,
as the city they surround
but barely comprehend.

VI

There's a city around this city.
In, it flows, and out again:
In electric grids
     and oil pipelines
     and air supplies
     and boiler parts;
in satellite dishes like rooftop mushrooms;
like bracket fungus stepping up the sides of concrete urban
    forests;
in highway truckers, convoys, road trains
bringing plastic flip-flops and computer chips.
In, it flows, and out again:
feeding, bleeding:
money, imports, spare supplies;
technicians, merchants, engineers.

VII

There's a city around this city:
A city of industry and landfills;
glass factories and furniture repairs;
a dying city, a trying city,
a city under attack, assault, explosions,
trading in mortar rounds, assassinations, and kidnappings;
hawking shortages, scandals, extraordinary efforts;
gambling for high stakes
on past profits
and future fears.

VIII

There's a city around this city,
the city where window glass rained down
to cover twenty urban city blocks
in a pyroclastic flow
of office trash, and smoke, and ash,
and screaming jumpers,
and burning fuels:
the haggard eyes of witnesses—
red-rimmed, blackened, staring,
fists balled, throats hoarse from shouting at the sky,
from begging God to stop the rain—
seen and wrapped around the globe;
surrounding all cities now.

Notes

Excavations is an extended reflection on how cities layer and blend past, present, and future throughout their construction and among their citizens.

Vienna was written while I was participating in arms control negotiations in Vienna, Austria, 1988–89. This was the time of "the Autumn of Nations" that culminated in the end of the Cold War and the beginning of a reunited Europe. During that time, I walked daily past major subway renovations that exposed archaeological layers dating back nearly two thousand years, including an entire medieval chapel. On May 2, 1989, Hungary began dismantling its border fence with Austria. On August 19, nearly one thousand people crossed over during a joyous border picnic. By the end of September, the city of Vienna declared that holders of any Eastern European passport could use public transportation and visit public museums free of charge, and more than thirty-thousand east-bloc tourists flooded the city, filling the squares above ground, and passing monuments preserved below ground as stops on the new subway line. Not all prospered. Many joined the burgeoning ranks of the (figurative and literal) underground labor force (Karlsplatz Underground), but the sense of exhuberance and rediscovery (of friends; of kin; of shared Vienna-Budapest-Prague culture) was (nearly) everywhere.

Berlin was written while commuting by rail to teach in outposts in and around that city in 1990. It records the sober mornings after the fall of the Wall on November 9, 1989. *Die Wende* (The Change), as it was known in Germany, tore down barriers to movement, but also tore down businesses and trade nets deemed unfit to participate in the New Economy; it reunited families, but also opened old wounds, revealed old secrets, and was followed by violent attacks against foreign workers and asylum seekers, housed in barracks in forgotten urban wastelands.

San Diego is a love poem to my hometown. It, like me, was and is shaped by the great ocean waves that bore and commingled immigrant waves from time immemorial with immigrant waves from Spain, and Italy, and through them (and subsequent to them) from the Middle East, North Africa, and a hundred other shores. To San Diego, great ships of exploration came across world oceans; from San Diego, great ships of war depart to patrol those selfsame seas. It is the city from which I have set out on great adventures, and to which I have always returned. It could be any port city, really: it reminds me most of Charleston, at the same latitude, on America's opposite shore.

Babylon is a fractured tour of multiple cities in the Middle East. It chronicles my reflections on the disintegration of the great promise of unification held out to Europe at the end of the Cold War. It was written while working on several projects aimed at bringing stability and hope to the part of the world that has inspired great writing and great religions since urban life began. As at the Tower of Babel, great achievement was undone by miscommunication, greed, and conflicting vision.

Baghdad was written while I worked on reconstruction projects in Iraq in 2003–4. The city still struggles to come to grips with its new present and old pasts. It is, in a very real sense, the successor city of the once-great Babylon. We hope that, like Vienna or Berlin, some new great city will arise from the rubble of war.

CPSIA information can be obtained at www.ICGtesting.com
Printed in the USA
LVOW091107271211

261197LV00002B/1/P